Problem so[lving]
and reasoning
workbook

This book belongs to

....

Colour the star when you complete a page.
See how far you've come!

Author: Tom Hall

How to use this book

- This workbook will help your child improve basic skills, build confidence and develop a love of learning.
- Find a quiet, comfortable place to work, away from distractions.
- Get into a routine of completing one or two workbook pages with your child every day.
- Ask your child to circle the star that matches how many questions they have completed every two pages:

Some = half of the questions   Most = more than half   All = all the questions

- Encourage your child to work through all of the questions eventually, and praise them for completing them.
- When your child has fully completed a page, ask them to colour in the relevant star on the first page of the book. This will enable you to keep track of progress through the activities and help to motivate your child.
- This book contains lots of problem-solving and reasoning activities for your child to complete. Your child will have to select and apply the appropriate number, measurement, and/or geometry and statistics skills to solve each problem.

> **Learning tip**
> Look out for tips on how to help your child.

- Encourage your child to break down the activities in order to work them out, and to make notes and drawings to help them.
- If your child is struggling with an activity, discuss with them what they know, what they need to find out and how they might go about it.
- Accessibility of content will be dependent on what your child has already covered in school and, at the lower age range in particular, your child may find some activities unfamiliar and/or very challenging. If so, leave them and move on, then revisit them at a later date.
- Ask your child to find, count and colour in the 15 little monkeys that are hidden throughout this book. This will help them engage with the pages of the book and get them interested in the activities.

(Don't count this one.)

Published by Collins
An imprint of HarperCollins*Publishers*
1 London Bridge Street
London SE1 9GF

HarperCollins*Publishers*
1st Floor, Watermarque Building, Ringsend Road,
Dublin 4, Ireland

First published 2020
This edition © HarperCollins*Publishers* 2022

10 9 8 7 6 5 4 3 2 1

ISBN 978-0-00-838790-7

The author asserts the moral right to be identified as the author of this work.

British Library Cataloguing in Publication Data

A catalogue record for this publication is available from the British Library.

Author: Tom Hall
Commissioning editor: Fiona McGlade
Text design and layout: Jouve India Private Limited and Contentra Technologies Limited
Illustrations: © HarperCollins*Publishers* and © Shutterstock.com
Cover design: Sarah Duxbury and Amparo Barrera
Project editor: Katie Galloway and Tracey Cowell
Production: Karen Nulty
Printed in India by Multivista Global Pvt. Ltd

Contents

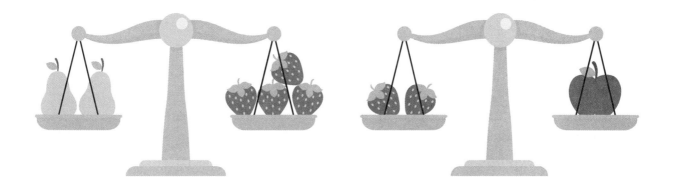

In the playground

1 Different paths are painted on the school playground.
They show numbers in different sequences.
Fill in the missing numbers.

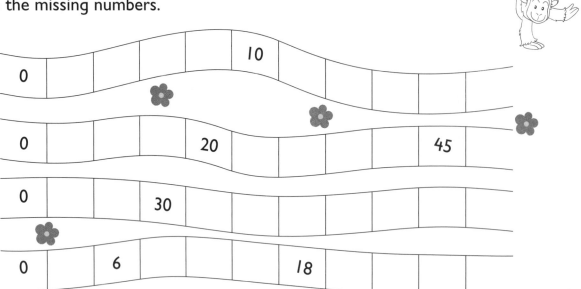

2 Ben and Dev lay ten hoops on the ground.

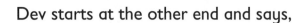

Ben starts at one end and says,

'I will move from one hoop to another,
counting forwards in **fives**, starting with **0**.'

Dev starts at the other end and says,

'I will move from one hoop to another,
counting backwards in **tens**, starting with **100**.'

Are these statements **true** or **false**? Circle the right answers.

Ben says, 'We will both say 50.'	**True**	**False**
Dev says, 'I will say 60, but Ben will not.'	**True**	**False**
Ben says, 'I will say 0, but Dev will not.'	**True**	**False**
Dev says, 'Neither of us will say 45.'	**True**	**False**
Ben says, 'We will both say 10.'	**True**	**False**

3 There are some items in the playground and a length is given to each one.

**swing
5 m**

**slide
4 m**

**bench
2 m**

**see-saw
3 m**

Put < or > in the circles to compare the length of the items.

swing ◯ see-saw   bench ◯ slide   swing ◯ bench

4 This number square is painted on the playground.

S	1	2	3	4	5
	10	9	8	7	6
	11	12	13	14	15
	20	19	18	17	16
	21	22	23	24	25

> **Learning tip**
> Remember, when counting on, children do not count the number they are on as one of the next numbers.

The children start at the square with the **S**.

Explain how you know these statements are correct.

Polly steps on all the multiples of 5. She will only step on numbers that are found at either end of a row.

_____

Ava steps on all the multiples of 2. She will **not** step on any odd numbers.

_____

Ali steps on every multiple of 10. There are 23 numbers on the square that he will **not** step on.

_____

How much did you do?

Circle the star to show how much you have done in activities 1–4.

Some   Most   All

Playing number games

1 Bilal is playing with six number cards.

| 3 tens | 2 ones | 7 tens | 9 ones | 6 tens | 5 ones |

Help Bilal use the cards to make the **smallest** 2-digit number.

Explain how you know you have made the smallest 2-digit number.

_____

_____

Explain why you cannot make the number **29** using these cards.

_____

_____

2 Fay and Max play a game with their number cards.
Write the numbers of Fay's cards on the blank cards to make **all** the number sentences correct.

Max's cards:

12 < [ ]

53 < [ ]

39 < [ ]

88 < [ ]

42 < [ ]

Fay's cards:

90   53

40   38

62

3 Nishi and Ben are playing a number game.
First, Nishi thinks of a number and Ben works out what it is.
Nishi says,

> 'The tens digit is an even number between 5 and 7.
> The ones digit is an odd number half the tens digit.'

What is Nishi's number? ☐

Learning tip
Talk through a problem, asking your child to use the facts that they are given to work out what answers **might** be.

Now Ben thinks of a number and Nishi works out what it is.
Ben says,

> 'My number has four ones and seven tens.'

What is Ben's number? ☐

4 Ben, Fay and Max are playing with abacuses.
What are the numbers shown on these abacuses?

A   B   C

T O   T O   T O

☐   ☐   ☐

Max uses **all** the beads on Abacus A to make a different number.
Write three different numbers that Max could make.

☐   ☐   ☐

Fay adds **three more** beads to Abacus B to make a different number.
Write three different numbers that Fay could make.

☐   ☐   ☐

How much did you do?

Circle the star to show how much you have
done in activities 1–4.

Some   Most   All

Using digit cards 1

1 Samir uses three blank cards.

How can Samir make a total of 20?

Fill in the blank cards below to find different ways.

An example is done for you.

| 1 | 1 | + | 9 | = 20 | | | + | | = 20 | | | + | | = 20 |

| | | + | | = 20 | | | + | | = 20 | | | + | | = 20 |

Samir uses the blank cards to show subtractions from 20.

Fill in the blank cards below to find different ways.

An example is done for you.

20 – | 1 | = | 1 | 9 | 20 – | | = | | | 20 – | | = | | |

20 – | | | = | | 20 – | | | = | | 20 – | | | = | |

2 Here are five digit cards.

| 1 | 3 | 5 | 7 | 9 |

Choose three of these cards that add up to the totals.

| | + | | + | | = 13 | | | + | | + | | = 19 |

| | + | | + | | = 15 | | | + | | + | | = 17 |

| | + | | + | | = 11 | | | + | | + | | = 21 |

3 Kara sets out some digit cards to show addition and subtraction calculations.

Some numbers are hidden.

Write the hidden numbers in the shaded boxes.

| 4 | | − | 1 | 6 | = 33 |

| 5 | 2 | + | 1 | | = 68 |

| | 8 | − | 4 | 6 | = 22 |

| 4 | 7 | + | | 1 | = 98 |

Learning tip
Remind your child to check carefully whether an addition symbol or a subtraction symbol is used.

4 Nisha has three digit cards.

| 4 | | 5 | | 6 |

Learning tip
Talk about what the answer is and how your child worked it out.

She arranges the cards to make an addition using a 2-digit number and a 1-digit number.

Use the cards to add up to the totals.

An example is done for you.

| 4 | 5 | + | 6 | = 51 | | | + | | = 60 | | | + | | = 69

Next, Nisha arranges the cards to subtract a 1-digit number from a 2-digit number.

Write the cards Nisha uses to give these differences.

| | | − | | = 48 | | | − | | = 52 | | | − | | = 59

How much did you do?

Circle the star to show how much you have done in activities 1–4.

Some   Most   All

Using digit cards 2

1 Olivia uses 20 blank cards to make an array:

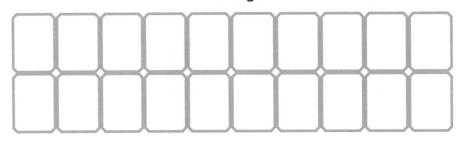

Make a different array using the same number of blank cards.

2 Tom arranges some digit cards to make three numbers:

| 2 | 5 | 1 | 0 |

He uses these three numbers to make two multiplication facts and two division facts.
Write the facts Tom makes.

_____   _____

_____   _____

Harry also arranges some digit cards to make three numbers.
Two of the cards are hidden.

| 2 | | | 2 | 0 |

Harry uses these three numbers to make two multiplication facts and two division facts.
Write the facts Harry makes, showing the hidden number.

Learning tip
Learning the multiplication facts (and division facts) for the 2, 5 and 10 times tables will really benefit your child.

_____   _____

_____   _____

3 These multiplication and division facts have a missing number.

Fill in the missing numbers to complete the facts.

7 × [ ] = 14   16 ÷ [ ] = 8   [ ][ ] × 5 = 50

[ ] × 5 = 20   [ ][ ] ÷ 10 = 6   10 ÷ [ ][ ] = 1

[ ][ ] ÷ 2 = 9   [ ][ ] ÷ 10 = 2   [ ] × 5 = 10

---

4 Jethro picks these number cards.

[2]   [3]   [5]   [6]   [8]   [0]

He uses some of these cards to make multiplication facts.

Use the cards to write the facts that have these answers.

[ ] × [ ] = 15   [ ] × [ ] = 30

[ ] × [ ] = 12   [ ] × [ ] = 16

Next, Jethro uses the cards to make some division facts.

He puts some cards together to make 2-digit numbers.

Use the cards to write the facts that have these answers.

[ ] ÷ [ ] = 2   [ ] ÷ [ ] = 4

[ ][ ] ÷ [ ] = 5   [ ][ ] ÷ [ ] = 6

Learning tip
Look at the answers and see if your child knows a fact with that answer. Can they find numbers on the cards to match the fact?

How much did you do?

Circle the star to show how much you have done in activities 1–4.

 Some   Most   All

At the toy shop

1 Sally buys 4 small teddy bears at the toy shop. She already has 5 medium-sized teddy bears and 7 large teddy bears.

How many teddy bears does she have altogether?

Gill has bought 16 toy cars. 3 are small cars and 8 are medium cars. The rest are large cars.

How many are large cars?

2 The toy shop has these teddy bears for sale.

The shop sells 16 teddy bears in one day.

Write a number sentence with the answer to show how many teddy bears are left.

_____

3 Jo counts 24 toy dinosaurs on three shelves in the shop.

There are 12 on the bottom shelf and 8 on the middle shelf.

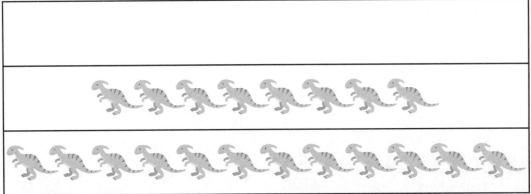

How many toy dinosaurs are on the top shelf?

4 The toy shop has 51 jigsaw puzzles for sale.

The shop owner orders another 30 jigsaw puzzles.

Complete the number sentence to show how many jigsaw puzzles are on sale now.

51 + ☐ = ☐

5 Hao buys 32 crayons and Jo buys 20 crayons.

Complete the number sentence to show how many more crayons Hao buys than Jo.

32 − ☐ = ☐

6 The shop sells kites. They come in blue, pink or green and can be large or small.

- There are 8 blue kites and 6 of them are small.
- There are 10 pink kites and 4 of them are small.
- There are 9 green kites and 4 of them are small.

How many **large** kites are there? ☐

7 Beth, Kate and Jess buy key rings.
Beth has 15 key rings. Kate has **7 more** than Beth. Jess has **3 less** than Kate.

How many key rings does Jess have? ☐

8 Fay has 12 bears. 6 of them wear only a hat. 2 of them wear only a jacket. The rest wear only a tie. Fay says,

'5 of the bears have a tie.'

Explain why Fay must be wrong.

_____

_____

How much did you do?

Circle the star to show how much you have done in activities 1–8.

 Some   Most   All

At the greengrocer's

1 Debbie runs a greengrocer.
She has a box of 50 apples.
She sells the apples in bags of 5

How many bags can Debbie fill?

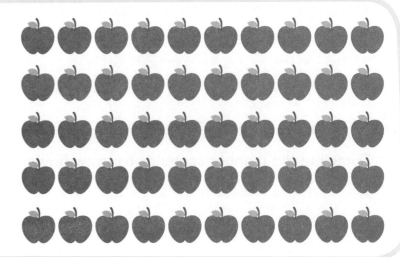

2 Debbie sells bananas in bunches of 5.
She sells 4 bunches.

How many bananas did she sell?

3 A box of cherries has 12 pairs of cherries and 16 single cherries.

How many cherries are there altogether in the box?

4 Debbie has 20 oranges.

Learning tip
For this question, encourage your child to group the oranges into twos; then into fives; then into tens by drawing around them in pencil.

She can sell them in twos. How many pairs will she sell?

She can sell them in fives. How many groups of five will she sell?

She can sell them in tens. How many groups of ten will she sell?

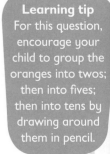

5 Debbie sells pears in bags of 5.

Each time she sells a bag, she makes a note of it.
This is her list:

5 + 5 + 5 + 5 + 5 + 5 + 5 + 5

How could Debbie write this as a multiplication?

Debbie also makes a note of other fruit she sells in the same way.
Write each of these as a multiplication.

2 + 2 + 2 + 2 + 2 + 2

10 + 10 + 10 + 10 + 10 + 10 + 10 + 10 + 10

Learning tip
Discuss with your child how addition and multiplication are related, e.g. 2 + 2 + 2 is the same as 2 x 3.

Learning tip
Use the multiplication facts that you and your child know, and discuss ways that these could be used.

6 Debbie receives a delivery of 12 boxes. Each box contains 5 coconuts.

She puts the coconuts on the shelves. Each shelf holds 10 coconuts.

How many shelves will be filled with coconuts?

Learning tip
Encourage your child to work through the question step by step, making notes as they go.

7 Debbie puts some fruit on the weighing scales.

| 2 pears | 4 strawberries | 2 strawberries | 1 apple | 2 pears | ? apples |

How many apples will have the same mass as 2 pears?

How much did you do?

Circle the star to show how much you have
done in activities 1–7.

Some   Most   All

Fun with flags

Learning tip
It is important that your child understands that halves and quarters of a shape or amount must be exactly the same.

1 Joe and his friends are making flags.
Joe says,

'My flag is half black and half white.'

Circle Joe's flag.

2 Here are four flags.

What fraction of these flags have a cross?

3 Theo draws four flags that all have stripes.
Circle the flag that is the odd one out.

  A   B   C   D

Explain why you think it is the odd one out.

_____

_____

4 These flags have been divided into four parts.

Tick the flag that is divided into quarters.

Explain how you know.

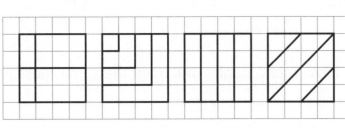

_____

_____

5 Here are five square flags drawn on a square grid.
Find different ways of splitting the flags in half.

6 Ola has a book of flags.
A quarter of the flags in the book are red. These are the red flags.

How many flags are in Ola's book **altogether**? [ ]

7 This flag is drawn on a square grid.

Tom says, 'I have divided the flag into quarters.'

Fay says, 'No, the shapes are different so they can't be quarters.'

Who is right? Explain why.

_____

_____

_____

How much did you do?

Circle the star to show how much you have done in activities 1–7.

 Some Most All

At the supermarket

1 This large jar holds the same amount of honey as the four small jars.

How many **small** jars hold the same as **2 large** jars?

How many **large** jars hold the same as **12 small** jars?

How many **small** jars will **half fill** the **large** jar?

How many **small** jars could be **half filled** by **1 large** jar?

2 This large bag of flour has the same mass as three small bags of flour.

Which is heavier: **2 large** bags or **4 small** bags? _____

Which is heavier: **8 small** bags or **3 large** bags? _____

How many **small** bags have the same mass as **4 large** bags?

How many **large** bags have the same mass as **6 small** bags?

3 This large block of butter is twice the length of a small block of butter.

Which is **longer**: **3 long** blocks or **5 short** blocks? _____

Which is **shorter**: **2 long** blocks or **5 short** blocks? _____

How many **short** blocks are the same as **3 long** blocks?

How many **long** blocks are the same as **10 short** blocks?

Learning tip
Drawing these problems will help your child to visualise the question.

4 Ben looks at some items in the supermarket.

Draw lines to match the items to their units of measure.

Potatoes		Metres
Juice		Kilograms
String		Litres

5 Leni compares the mass of some items she buys.
Use **>**, **<** or **=** to compare the masses.

tomatoes 300 grams ☐ jam 300 grams | grapes 200 grams ☐ eggs 200 grams | pineapple 1 kilogram ☐ cheese $\frac{1}{2}$ kilogram

6 Mia measures the length of some of the green beans that she bought.
This ruler measures in centimetres.

B

A

0 1 2 3 4 5 6 7 8 9 10

How long is bean A? ☐   How long is bean B? ☐

Learning tip
Make sure that your child practises using a ruler.

7 Nico buys a 5-litre bottle of water. He pours some of the water into glasses that each hold 1 litre. The picture shows what is left in the bottle.

How many glasses did Nico fill? ☐

How much water is left in the bottle? ☐

5

litres

0

8 Lily buys 1 kilogram of pears. What will she use to weigh them?
Circle your answer.

ruler   jug   scales   thermometer

How much did you do?

Circle the star to show how much you have done in activities 1–8.

☆ Some   ★ Most   ★ All

Pocket money

1 Ranjeet is counting his pocket money. He has six different coins.
Number the coins **1–6** to help Ranjeet put them in order. Start with the coin with the least value.

2 Katie wants to buy five different items with five different coins or notes.
Draw a line from each item to the coin or note that Katie will use.
(Use each coin/note only once.)

70p   45p   £1.75   £3   20p

3 Jack wants to use some pocket money to buy an apple for 25p and an orange for 30p.

He has six 10p coins.

How much money will he have left after buying an apple and an orange?

4 Toby, Ben, Mo and Jack count their pocket money.
How much does each boy have?

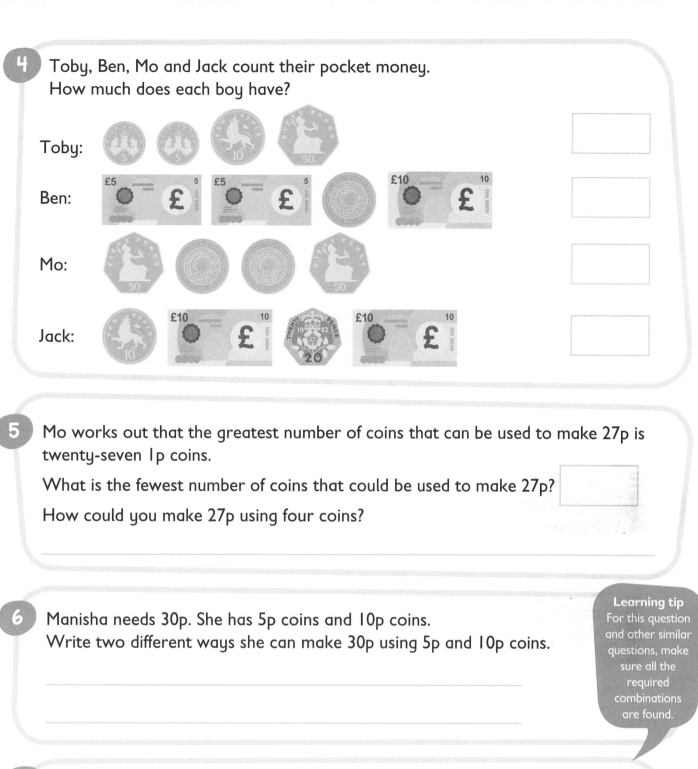

Toby: ☐

Ben: ☐

Mo: ☐

Jack: ☐

---

5 Mo works out that the greatest number of coins that can be used to make 27p is twenty-seven 1p coins.

What is the fewest number of coins that could be used to make 27p? ☐

How could you make 27p using four coins?

_____

Learning tip
For this question and other similar questions, make sure all the required combinations are found.

6 Manisha needs 30p. She has 5p coins and 10p coins.
Write two different ways she can make 30p using 5p and 10p coins.

_____

_____

---

7 Ben wants to spend his pocket money on a trip to the cinema. An adult ticket costs £10 and a children's ticket costs £5.

• How many adult tickets can Ben buy with £40? ☐

• How many children's tickets can he buy with £40? ☐

How much did you do?

Circle the star to show how much you have done in activities 1–7.

Some   Most   All

At the railway station

1 Beth catches a train at half past 9.
Which clock shows half past 9? Tick the correct clock.

Tom's train left 5 minutes after Beth's train.
Which clock shows the time Tom's train left? Tick the correct clock.

2 This clock shows when Sam's train leaves. Circle the time Sam's train leaves.

10 to 1	5 to 10
10 past 1	5 past 10

3 Nadia gets on a train on Thursday. She says,

'I will come back tomorrow.'

What day does Nadia come back? _____

4 Three friends are taking different trains to town.
- Javid's train takes 1 hour.
- Harry's train takes 45 minutes.
- Lucy's train takes $\frac{1}{2}$ an hour.

Write the names of the friends in order of journey time. Start with the friend whose train takes the shortest time.

_____ _____ _____

5 The clock at the railway station has the minute hand missing.

Nisha's train leaves at 5 to 3.
Will Nisha be in time for her train?
Explain your answer.

_____

_____

Learning tip
Check that your child knows how many minutes there are in:
- an hour
- a quarter of an hour
- half an hour
- three-quarters of an hour.

6 Amil is on a train that set off at half past 8. The journey takes 1 hour.
He looks at his watch and the time is quarter past 9.
How many more minutes is it before Amil's train arrives?

7 The clocks show the times that three trains leave a station, and the times that they arrive at their destination.

Train 1
leaves at   and arrives at

Train 2
leaves at   and arrives at

Train 3
leaves at   and arrives at

Write the trains in order, starting with the train that takes the shortest time.

How much did you do?

Circle the star to show how much you have done in activities 1–7.

 Some   Most   All

Sorting shapes

1 Ivan is doing some drawing. He draws these four shapes.

A   B   C   D

Learning tip Discuss the properties of 2-D and 3-D shapes, so that your child can distinguish between individual shapes.

Which shape is the square? Explain how you know.

_____

_____

Ivan says,

'I have drawn two rectangles.'

Is Ivan correct? Explain the reason for your answer.

_____

_____

2 Ria pulls these 3-D shapes from the toy box.

A   B   C   D

Which shape is the pyramid? Explain how you know.

_____

_____

Ria says,

'I have got two cuboids out of the toy box.'

Is Ria correct? Explain the reason for your answer.

_____

3 Emily takes some shapes and puts them into a sorting diagram.

	_____ sided shapes	Not four-sided shapes
_____ sides only	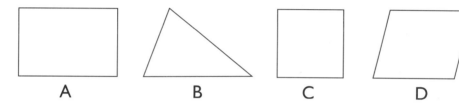	
Some curved sides		

What word and number are missing from the sorting diagram?
Fill them in.
If Emily added a square to the diagram, where would she put it?
Draw the square in the correct place.

4 Samir draws some 2-D shapes.

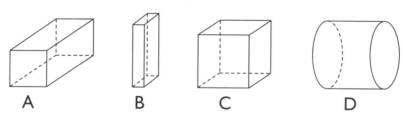

A   B   C   D

Which shape is the odd one out? Explain your answer.

_____

_____

Samir finds some shape blocks in the toy box.

A   B   C   D

Which shape is the odd one out? Explain your answer.

_____

_____

How much did you do?

Circle the star to show how much you have done in activities 1–4.

Some   Most   All

Reading a treasure map

Finn finds a treasure map.

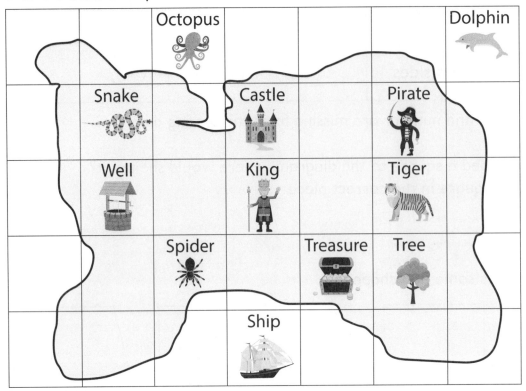

1. What is below the snake? _____

   What is above the king? _____

   What is to the left of the treasure? _____

   What is to the right of the well? _____

2. The king is facing the ship. He makes a half turn clockwise.

   What will he be facing? _____
   The pirate is facing the castle. He makes a three-quarter turn clockwise.

   What will he be facing? _____
   The snake is facing the castle. It makes a three-quarter turn anti-clockwise.

   What will it be facing? _____
   The tiger is facing the king. It makes a three-quarter turn anti-clockwise.

   What will it be facing? _____

3 The pirate moves one square left and two squares down.

What will he find? _____

The snake moves four squares right and two squares down.

Where will it be? _____

The tiger moves three squares left and two squares up.

What will it find? _____

Learning tip
Check that your child does not start counting from the square they start in.

4 The spider turns one right angle anti-clockwise and moves one square forward.

How many more squares will the spider have to move to reach the tree? ☐

The tiger moves three squares left.
How many right-angles to the right will it have to turn to see the king? ☐

Learning tip
Check your child understands what a right-angle is and that one right-angle is the same as one quarter turn.

5 What directions would the snake take to reach the spider?

_____

What directions would the dolphin take to reach the ship?

_____

6 Joe and Nishi look at the map. On the map, the king is facing the ship.

Joe says,

'The king turns to look at the well, so he is turning one right-angle to his right.'

Learning tip
For this question, compare turning right and left for your child and for another child standing opposite.

Nishi says, 'No, he is turning three right-angles to his left.'

Who do you think is right?

_____

How much did you do?

Circle the star to show how much you have done in activities 1–6.

Some   Most   All

At the library

This pictogram shows the number of books in the library read by a group of children.

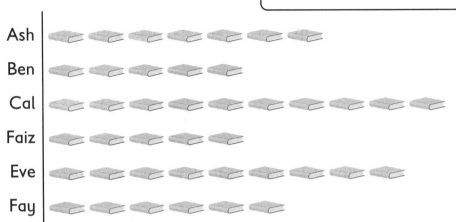

stands for 1 book

Ash
Ben
Cal
Faiz
Eve
Fay

Learning tip
If your child feels confident about this activity, discuss using a pictogram where one book symbol might stand for two books.

---

1 How many books did Eve read? ▢

Who read the same number of books as Ben? _____

---

2 How many more books did Ash read than Faiz? ▢

Who read two more books than Ash? _____

Who read four fewer books than Cal? _____

---

3 When a child has read 10 books they get a certificate.

How many children have a certificate? ▢

How many more books does Ben need to read to get a certificate? ▢

How much did you do?

Circle the star to show how much you have done in activities 1–3.

Some   Most   All

Sports day

On Sports day, three teams collect points. The team with the most points wins.

These block diagrams show the points after 10 races, and the points at the end of the day after 20 races.

Points after **10 races**

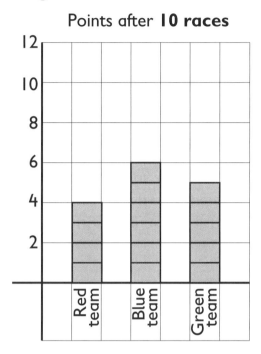

Points after **20 races**

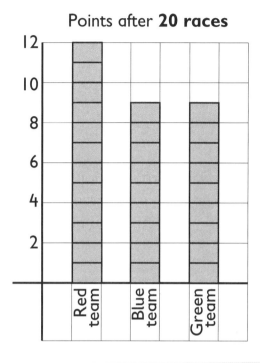

Learning tip
Make sure your child understands the value of the points between the numbers on the y-axis.

1 Which team was in the lead after 10 races? _____

How many points did the Green team have after 20 races? ☐

2 After 10 races, how many more points did the Blue team have than the Red team? ☐

After 20 races, how many fewer points did the Blue team have than the Red team? ☐

How many more points did the Red team have after 20 races than 10 races? ☐

How much did you do?

Circle the star to show how much you have done in activities 1–2.

Some   Most   All

Art club

This table gives some information about children in an art club.

| Class I | | | | Likes | |
Name		Age	Painting	Pottery	Craft
Tammy	Girl	6	✓	✓	
Ben	Boy	7		✓	✓
Bobby	Boy	7	✓	✓	
Dev	Boy	6			✓
Lily	Girl	7	✓	✓	✓
Polly	Girl	6	✓	✓	
Jack	Boy	6		✓	✓
Aleena	Girl	7	✓		✓
Tom	Boy	7		✓	✓
Max	Boy	7	✓	✓	✓

1 How many of the children are 6 years old? ☐

How many children like painting and pottery, but don't like craft? ☐

How many more children like pottery than like painting? ☐

2 This table shows the children in the school art club.
Complete the table.

	Class I	Class 2	Class 3	Total
Boys	6	_____	5	**17**
Girls	4	_____	3	_____
Total	_____	_____	_____	**32**

Learning tip
Tell your child to begin by finding the missing values where there is only one that is unknown in a column or row.

How much did you do?

Circle the star to show how much you have done in activities 1–2.

Some   Most   All

Answers

In the playground

1. 0 **2 4 6 8** 10 **12 14 16 18 20**
   0 **5 10 15** 20 **25 30 35 40** 45 **50**
   0 **10 20** 30 **40 50 60 70 80 90 100**
   0 **3 6 9 12 15** 18 **21 24 27 30**
2. False; True; True; False; True
3. swing > see-saw; bench < slide;
   swing > bench
4. The multiples of 5 are 5, 10, 15, 20 and
   25 and these are at the end of rows.
   Multiples of 2 are always even numbers.
   There are two multiples of 10, and 25
   numbers altogether, so 23 of the
   numbers are not multiples of 10.

Playing number games

1. 32; 3 is the smallest tens and 2 is the
   smallest ones.
   2 needs to be tens in the number 29 and
   there is no card for 2 tens.
2. 12 < 38; 53 < 62; 39 < 40; 88 < 90; 42 < 53
3. 63; 74
4. A = 34, B = 46, C = 25
   Three from: 70, 61, 52, 43, 25, 16, 7
   Three from: 94, 85, 76, 67, 58, 49

Using digit cards 1

1. **Five from:** 12 + 8 = 20; 13 + 7 = 20;
   14 + 6 = 20; 15 + 5 = 20; 16 + 4 = 20;
   17 + 3 = 20; 18 + 2 = 20; 19 + 1 = 20;
   20 + 0 = 20
   Two from: 20 − 2 = 18; 20 − 3 = 17;
   20 − 4 = 16; 20 − 5 = 15; 20 − 6 = 14;
   20 − 7 = 13; 20 − 8 = 12; 20 − 9 = 11;
   20 − 0 = 20
   Three from: (20 −10 = 10); 20 − 11 = 9;
   20 − 12 = 8; 20 − 13 = 7; 20 − 14 = 6;
   20 − 15 = 5; 20 − 16 = 4; 20 − 17 = 3;
   20 − 18 = 2; 20 − 19 = 1; 20 − 20 = 0
2. Additions can be written in any order.
   9 + 3 + 1 = 13 **OR** 7 + 5 + 1 = 13
   9 + 7 + 3 = 19
   9 + 5 + 1 = 15 **OR** 7 + 5 + 3 = 15
   9 + 5 + 3 = 17 **OR** 9 + 7 + 1 = 17
   7 + 3 + 1 = 11; 9 + 7 + 5 = 21

3. 49 − 16 = 33   52 + 16 = 68
   68 − 46 = 22   47 + 51 = 98
4. 54 + 6 = 60 **OR** 56 + 4 = 60
   65 + 4 = 69 **OR** 64 + 5 = 69
   54 − 6 = 48   56 − 4 = 52
   64 − 5 = 59

Using digit cards 2

1. Accept any of the following arrays:
   1 × 20 **OR** 20 × 1 **OR** 4 × 5 **OR** 5 × 4
2. 2 × 5 = 10; 5 × 2 = 10; 10 ÷ 2 = 5;
   10 ÷ 5 = 2
   2 × 10 = 20; 10 × 2 = 20;
   20 ÷ 2 = 10; 20 ÷ 10 = 2 **OR** 2 × 20 = 40;
   20 × 2 = 40; 40 ÷ 2 = 20; 40 ÷ 20 = 2
3. 7 × 2 = 14; 16 ÷ 2 = 8; **10** × 5 = 50;
   4 × 5 = 20; **60** ÷ 10 = 6; 10 ÷ **10** = 1;
   18 ÷ 2 = 9; **20** ÷ 10 = 2; **2** × 5 = 10
4. **3 × 5 = 15 OR 5 × 3 = 15;**
   5 × 6 = 30 OR 6 × 5 = 30;
   2 × 6 = 12 OR 6 × 2 = 12;
   2 × 8 = 16 OR 8 × 2 = 16
   6 ÷ 3 = 2; 8 ÷ 2 = 4; 30 ÷ 6 = 5; 30 ÷ 5 = 6

At the toy shop

1. 16 (teddy bears); 5 (large toy cars)
2. 30 − 16 = 14   3. 4 (dinosaurs)
4. 51 + **30** = **81**   5. 32 − **20** = **12**
6. 13 (large kites)   7. 19 (key rings)
8. Accept a correct calculation that shows
   the statement is incorrect, e.g. 6 + 2 = 8
   and 12 − 8 = 4, so there can't be 5.

At the greengrocer's

1. 10 (bags)   2. 20 (bananas);
3. 40 (cherries)   4. 10 (pairs);
   4 (groups of five); 2 (groups of ten)
5. 5 × 8 **OR** 8 × 5; 2 × 6 **OR** 6 × 2; 10 × 9
   OR 9 × 10
6. 6 (shelves)   7. 2 (apples)

Fun with flags

1.

2. $\frac{1}{4}$

3. D. It is the only one that is half shaded (the others are divided into thirds). **OR** any other correct explanation.
4. 3ʳᵈ flag ✓. It is the only flag divided into four **equal** parts.
5. Any ways of dividing the flags into two **equal** parts, e.g.

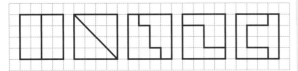

6. 12 (flags)
7. Tom is right. Each quarter is the same size. **OR** Each quarter has four small squares.

At the supermarket

1. 8 (small jars); 3 (large jars); 2 (small jars); 8 (small jars)
2. 2 (large bags); 3 (large bags); 12 (small bags); 2 (large bags)
3. 3 (long blocks); 2 (long blocks); 6 (short blocks); 5 (long blocks)
4. Potatoes – Kilograms; Juice – Litres; String – Metres
5. tomatoes = jam; grapes = eggs; pineapple > cheese
6. A = 6 cm; B = 8 cm
7. 2 (glasses); 3 (litres)
8. scales

Pocket money

1. 5p = **1**; 20p = **3**; £1 = **5**; 50p = **4**; £2 = **6**; 10p = **2**

2.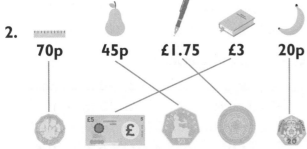

3. 5p
4. Toby 70p; Ben £22; Mo £5; Jack £20.30
5. Three (20p, 5p and 2p)
   Four coins: 10p, 10p, 5p, 2p **OR** 20p, 5p, 1p, 1p
6. 10p, 10p, 10p **OR** 10p, 10p, 5p, 5p **OR** 10p, 5p, 5p, 5p, 5p **OR** 5p, 5p, 5p, 5p, 5p, 5p
7. 4 (adult tickets); 8 (child tickets)

At the railway station

1. 3ʳᵈ clock ✓; 3ʳᵈ clock ✓   2. 5 past 10
3. Friday   4. Lucy, Harry, Javid
5. Yes. Time is about half past two/the minute hand is not just before 3 o'clock.
6. 15 (minutes)
7. Train 2, Train 3, Train 1

Sorting shapes

1. C. The square has four equal sides **AND** four right angles.
   Yes. A square is also a rectangle.
2. B. The shape has a 'base' and sides that come to a 'point' **OR** there is a 'base' and sides that are triangles.
   Yes. A cube is also a cuboid.
3. straight; four/4
   'Square' added to the top middle cell
4. B. The triangle is the only shape with three sides.
   D. The cylinder is the only shape with a curved side/only 3 sides.

Reading a treasure map

1. well; castle; spider; king **OR** tiger
2. castle; tiger **OR** tree; well; pirate
3. treasure; tree; octopus
4. 2 (squares); 2 (right angles)
5. 1 square right and 2 squares down; 4 squares down and 3 squares left;
6. Both are right.

At the library

1. 9 (books); Faiz
2. 2 (books); Eve; Fay
3. 1 (child); 5 (books)

Sports day

1. Blue team; 9 (points)
2. 2 (points); 3 (points); 8 (points)

Art club

1. 4 (children); 3 (children); 2 (children)
2.

	Class 1	Class 2	Class 3	Total
Boys	6	6	5	17
Girls	4	8	3	**15**
Total	**10**	**14**	**8**	32